PRAYING WITH THE WORD

Lent, Holy Week and Easter

DAVID HAAS

ST. ANTHONY MESSENGER PRESS

Cincinnati, Ohio

Nihil Obstat: Rev. Hilarion Kistner, O.F.M.
Rev. Ralph J. Lawrence
Imprimi Potest: Rev. John Bok, O.F.M., Provincial
Imprimatur: Most Reverend Carl K. Moeddel, V.G.
Archdiocese of Cincinnati, December 30, 1996
The *nihil obstat* and *imprimatur* are a declaration that a book
is considered to be free from doctrinal or moral error. It is
not implied that those who have granted the *nihil obstat* and
imprimatur agree with the contents, opinions or statements
expressed.

Scripture citations are taken from the *New Revised Standard
Version Bible*, copyright ©1989 by the Division of Christian
Education of the National Council of the Churches of Christ
in the U.S.A. and used by permission.

Cover design and illustrations by Karla Ripley
Book design by Mary Alfieri
Electronic format and pagination by Sandra Digman

ISBN 0-86716-300-3

Published by St. Anthony Messenger Press
Printed in the U.S.A.

Contents

To JEAN BROSS,
  friend and partner
    in ministry,
  seeker of possibilities,
    artist, dreamer
  and woman of faith—
    with love and gratitude

Acknowledgments

I want to thank the people of St. Anthony
Messenger Press, who are a joy to work with. I
am grateful for their support, especially that of
editor Lisa Biedenbach, who encouraged and
urged me to write these prayers.

I express my thankfulness to Sister Kathleen
Storms, S.S.N.D., who walked with me along
both fun and lonely roads and helped me to
unlock the spiritual conversation stirring within.

I also thank dear friends Rob and Mary
Glover, for their tenderness and acceptance and
for wrapping me into the fabric and love of their
family; faithful friends Barbara Colliander, Mary
Werner, Dan Kantor, Jim Bessert, Jo Infante, Pam
Cole, Mel and Therese Harvey, and Mary Jane

Moore; and Bob Piercy, Jean Bross, Kate Cuddy, David Fischer, Derek Campbell and Patty Stromen for their gifts, their friendship and their partnership with me in ministry.

Also, I am grateful to dear friends Art Zannoni, Bill Huebsch and Betsey Beckman for their vision and the inspiration of their writing, insights and wisdom; and to the associates of The Emmaus Center for Music, Prayer, and Ministry, who truly give me hope and delight.

Finally, I thank Helen for loving me in the midst of emotional and creative ups and downs, and my parents for their love and care for me and their untiring energy and passion for all that is good in life.

Introduction

Lent has always been a difficult time for my
father. During my growing-up years, I saw Dad's
mood begin to change to dread as the weather
became drearier and Ash Wednesday drew
nearer on the calendar. To me and to those who
know him well, Dad is the consummate Easter
person—optimistic and life-giving. He always
sees life in the midst of difficult and painful
situations and encourages our family members
and others to see the best in all things. Dad's is a
nurturing presence: creative, open, seeing hope
and possibility amid the most paradoxical and
fateful circumstances.

For him and for many of his generation, Lent
was (and still seems to be) a conspiracy to shatter

happiness and hope, a time to focus on our sinfulness and our lack of possibilities, a time to remember and instill in ourselves self-loathing and hopelessness.

Some of Dad's resistance to Lent actually taught me more about the season's true meaning and purpose. I believe strongly that his wonderful optimistic outlook on the possibilities of our existence is actually the corrective way to look at this season: Lent is not a time of darkness and nothingness, but rather the eternal springtime of hope on the spiritual path we all travel. The linking of Lent and Easter is the ultimate mystery of our faith. It embodies the "yin-yang" of our lives, teaching us that we cannot have one without the other.

Certainly, Lent calls us to examine evil, to take inventory, to scrutinize and repent, but to do so in the context that there is a God who walks with us, that healing is not only a possibility but actually God's promise for us.

We examine our lives with the trust and hope that something lies better on the other side. Lent should be for us a time to embrace and welcome the opportunity for growth and to come to know God, ourselves and each other in a fresh and vibrant way. Scripture proclaims this:

> "At an acceptable time I have listened to you,
> and on the day of salvation I have helped you."
> See, now is the acceptable time; see, now is the

day of salvation! (2 Corinthians 6:2-3)

The time is fulfilled, and the kingdom of God
has come near;... (Mark 1:15)

What then are we to say about these things? If
God is for us, who is against us? (Romans 8:31)

Therefore, since we are justified by faith, we
have peace with God through our Lord Jesus
Christ, through whom we have obtained access
to this grace in which we stand; and we boast in
our hope of sharing the glory of God.
(Romans 5:1-2)

"Quickly, bring out a robe—the best one—and
put it on him; put a ring on his finger and
sandals on his feet...let us eat and celebrate; for
this son of mine was dead and is alive again; he
was lost and is found!" And they began to
celebrate. (Luke 15:22-24)

I am the resurrection and the life. Those who
believe in me, even though they die, will live,
and everyone who lives and believes in me will
never die. (John 11:25-26)

"Woman, where are they? Has no one
condemned you?" She said, "No one, sir." And
Jesus said, "Neither do I condemn you."
(John 8:10-11)

While pain and growth lie at the heart of the
Lenten conversion journey, these Scripture

passages and many others proclaimed during this season are filled with the message of salvation and redemption, of life in the midst of death, of hope in the midst of hopelessness. These exhortations and stories found in the Lenten canon are filled with the promise proclaimed and fulfilled when we follow Jesus Christ: Death will not win; it will not be our destiny.

Easter, while joyous, of course, does not mean only singing, dancing and rejoicing. The Resurrection brings responsibility and the reminder of what it takes to get to the empty tomb. Easter demands a response, not only in words and joyful singing, but in a change to a new way of being and living, to a true conversion that occurs daily and is not always happy, is often painful and is, sometimes, even boring.

How to Use This Book

I created this collection of seasonal prayers as a companion on the journey through the Paschal season. Each of us has a unique approach to prayer and dialogue with God. My prayer style is conversational, so the prayers here reflect my personal journey of growth and path toward the Holy One. These prayers are grounded in my experience and the many faith questions I both celebrate and struggle with.

For each day of Lent, Holy Week and Easter, you will find listed the Scripture passage as found in the Lectionary, followed by a prayerful reflection upon that word.

After dwelling on the Scripture for the day, I reflected upon my personal life and how I am affected when hearing the passage. Then I stated before God that which God already knows—my present situation. I placed myself before God's power and care for me, with a plea or acknowledgment of my dependence upon God. I concluded each prayer with a commitment to action, a goal or intention to live the word with integrity, through my words and actions.

These prayers will find their fullness when prayed alongside the Scripture assigned for the day. The prayers do not replace Scripture but enrich it. I intend them for your own personal spiritual nurturing, not as liturgical prayers or orations for public worship. You might consider the prayers a touchstone to pray with the Bible during the ninety days of Lent, Holy Week and Easter. Small faith-sharing groups, retreatants and those preparing for initiation into the Church at Easter may find this book useful, too, during this time of purification and enlightenment.

My hope is that all who pray with these prayers can come to know more deeply the power of God's word and integrate that message into daily life. I wrote out of my own discovery that God is in charge and that I need only to listen well and then respond honestly in my heart and with how I live my life.

May this time of Lent, Holy Week and Easter call each of us to a deeper conversion in our lives and help bring us all closer to the promise of Christ.

David Haas
The Emmaus Center for Music, Prayer, and Ministry

Ash Wednesday

Joel 2:12-18
Psalm 51:3-4, 5-6, 12-13, 14, 17
2 Corinthians 5:20—6:2
Matthew 6:1-6, 16-18

God,
once again—
for it is certainly not the first time—
you call me to return to the center that is you,
to your place,
to your way of doing things.

You have asked me many times
to come back to the place where you dwell,
to listen only to you,
to focus on you,
to live intimately with you.

So here I am again,
hoping that this time
your word will take hold
and find a home within me.

Here and now, God,
I recommit myself to you,
to find space and time to pray
and to not conveniently forget.

I promise again
to be closely in touch with you.

I reverence again your call to fast
and not just "give up things."
I want to fast from
all that is negative,
all that does me and others harm:
greed, whining, selfishness,
self-indulgence, destructive behavior.

I want to be centered
in the praise of others,
to find joy in other people's victories
(and mine as well),
to revel in your goodness
and the wonderful springtime
that is you alone.

Instead of giving up,
I want to "take on,"
to choose not to live
in guilt and shame,
for that is not you.
I want to celebrate
and take on a new way,
to begin a renewal
within myself.
I want to make a difference, Lord,

not just during this time of Lent,
but for all my time.
I want to begin a new way of living
that echoes your call to each of us
to serve your children everywhere.

I promise to go outside myself
to be with someone who is lonely,
who is dying of AIDS,
who is hurting from a broken relationship.
I will visit those imprisoned,
feed those who are hungry,
fight for those who are oppressed
and who suffer.
In their eyes and in their stories,
I hope to see myself.
Together may we experience healing—
not necessarily a cure—
a balm that will anoint us with the hope
that your rising is not something
only to remember nostalgically
as a wonderful historical story
but as your promise for each of us.

Help me and all my sisters and brothers
return to you.
For now is the time. Now. Amen.

Thursday After Ash Wednesday

Deuteronomy 30:15-20
Psalm 1:1-2, 3, 4, 6
Luke 9:22-25

God,
you do not manipulate us,
or force us into submission,
or trick us to see things your way.

You give us choices.
You make it hard.
It would be so much easier
if you would simply
lead us to the right door,
find the key
and open it for us.

But you choose a different strategy.
You lay out the choices,
not simple ones,
but direct nevertheless.
"Life and death."
This choice means
we have to take on
and wear with dignity
the instrument of death—
your cross, our cross.

4

I don't like this path.
I don't want demands placed upon me.
I feel that I have suffered enough
and made enough sacrifices.
But you keep asking me
to make the choice.

Can't you see how I have blundered?
I continue to make bad choices,
the wrong choices,
choices that lead me
away from my best self,
the self that you have
intended me to be.
I keep harming others
and myself as well.
Too often I am seduced
by my own self-destructiveness
and I end up alone, ashamed.

Sometimes I question your thinking, God.
How can you keep coming back to me,
keep laying out the choices,
when I continue to make bad choices?
Yet, each time I choose unwisely,
you say to me,
without losing your temper and patience,
"Choose again."

Walk with me, God,
and help me muster the courage
to choose well,
to take up your cross
and to trust that you will never abandon me.
Guide me and then the cross
will not be so heavy.
Then I will be able to see
that I can choose better—
for myself,
for others
and for you. Amen.

Friday After Ash Wednesday

Isaiah 58:1-9
Psalm 51:3-4, 5-6, 18-19
Matthew 9:14-15

God,
I hate to feel insecure.
I have many things all around me
that keep me from feeling unsafe.

At least I think so most of the time.

It is amazing
that the more "stuff" I acquire
and the more I buy,
the more I am still frightened
and isolated from seeing
the poor and less fortunate
around me.

I feel guilty then
because when I take inventory
not just of all that I possess
but of the quality of the life I live,
I wonder how I have deserved
to be so blessed,
so comfortable,
so free from worry about

what I am to eat or wear
or where I will sleep tonight.

I can usually find a way out
of my feelings of guilt
by praying fervently
for the poor and hungry,
by saying all the right things
at the right times,
by moving away from unpleasantness,
by sending a check and patting myself
on the back for my generosity.

But the poor and the hungry
still stand around me.
Their cries get louder,
and my attempts to run the other way
catch up with me,
and I find myself out of breath
and out of excuses.

God,
today I will share my bread,
I will visit the homeless shelter
to welcome the stranger
and find out what I can do
to make a difference
in someone else's life.

In your loving care
may my voice and my life
become a trumpet blast,
heralding and proclaiming to the world
that there is bread
and hope for all.
Help me to act. Amen.

Saturday After Ash Wednesday

Isaiah 58:9-14
Psalm 86:1-2, 3-4, 5-6
Luke 5:27-32

God,
I often dwell
(far too much I'm afraid)
on how other people see me
and describe me to others,
on the qualities that some say
are evident within me.
I am selfish and narcissistic at times,
caught up in what others think of me.
People tell me I should not be
so concerned about what others think,
but rather, what I think of myself.

How do I see myself?
What descriptive phrase will be etched
on my gravestone?
What will be my legacy?
Will I be remembered as a shining light?
Will I be remembered as a "breach-mender"
or a "restorer of ruined houses"?
Will I be seen as one who delighted not in gossip
but who celebrated life with goodness
and delight?

Help me, God,
to be freed from these obsessions
and the compulsive worry about my reputation,
my standing with others, my integrity.
Free me to stay focused on you
and embrace the implications
of what that means.
Help me to leave my life in your hands
and invest totally in you
so all the rest will be taken care of.

Help me let go
and simply follow you. Amen.

First Sunday of Lent

(A) *Genesis 2:7-9; 3:1-7*
   Psalm 51:3-4, 5-6, 12-13, 14, 17
   Romans 5:12-19
   Matthew 4:1-11

(B) *Genesis 9:8-15*
   Psalm 25:4-5, 6-7, 8-9
   1 Peter 3:18-22
   Mark 1:12-15

(C) *Deuteronomy 26:4-10*
   Psalm 91:1-2, 10-11, 12-13, 14-15
   Romans 10:8-13
   Luke 4:1-13

God,
you loom above and beyond
all things in my life.
I start with you,
I end with you,
and you are everything in-between.

You give me this time
of retreat and reflection
to seize the gift
that you have waiting for me.

You promise not a sword
but healing for my wounds.
You promise me an adventure
not of death and endings
but an honest and fair obstacle course—
that you run with me—
that leads to a profound reward.

This is the time of fulfillment,
of possibilities,
of completion.

Help me hear your word
and remember that you do not tempt me
but hold out for me a more beautiful way,
filled with life to the full.

May my life today flow from your cross
and my heart be filled anew.
May I dwell with you in all things.
Be with me when I am in trouble
and raise me up with you. Amen.

Monday of the First Week of Lent

Leviticus 19:1-2, 11-18
Psalm 19:8, 9, 10, 15
Matthew 25:31-46

God,
I can't speak for others,
but when I am honest with myself,
I admit that I look for
the easiest path to be good
and for every possible shortcut
when the goal seems too big
or too risky.

With you there can be no shortcuts.
You call all of us to go outside ourselves,
to be inconvenienced for each other,
to take the uphill climb
in the journey with you.

Your way is the way of justice,
not charity alone.
Your way means to uncover,
name and call evil
all that lies at the root of hunger,
violence, injustice and hatred.
Your way means to respond,
not temporarily during this season,

but during our entire lives.
You challenge us to take no shortcuts,
no sabbatical for doing good deeds,
but to transform ourselves
and live in obedience and celebration
of the vision of your new world.

The life that you have promised
to all of us
is not a distant possibility or dream.
Give us the courage
and the sense to travel
the difficult and bumpy road,
to endure the ride
and arrive at the sweet destination
of your justice. Amen.

Tuesday of the First Week of Lent

Isaiah 55:10-11
Psalm 34:4-5, 6-7, 16-17, 18-19
Matthew 6:7-15

God,
there are times when the
unpredictability of the weather
drives me crazy.
Where I live,
rain and snow come unexpectedly.
I do not like to brave the elements.
I'd rather watch from my window inside.
It's warm here; it's safe here;
here it's without risk.

You might find it fascinating to know
(of course you already know, you're God!)
that when it rains hard
and I must get to my car outside,
I run like a demon
because I have again misplaced my umbrella.
I try not to get wet;
I don't want the rain to touch me.
But, of course, the rain—
your rain—
catches me.

Your word and your voice
are like that rain.
You keep after me,
even when I think I can escape
the gentle yet piercing message
eternally "raining" in my ears
and in my heart.

When I listen well,
your rain—
or, pardon the pun, your "reign"—
waters my soul,
nurtures my heart
and flowers my life.
The blossoms then become
the everlasting intention
of your call:
compassion, healing,
unconditional love and forgiveness.

Help me remember
to linger and take my time
while I'm in the rain.
If I move too fast,
I may step carelessly in your garden
and miss the colors. Amen.

Wednesday of the First Week of Lent

Jonah 3:1-10
Psalm 51:3-4, 12-13, 18-19
Luke 11:29-32

God,
it can be easy to lose one's optimism,
to despair and dwell in hopelessness.
There is so much pain
in our world,
in our families,
in our relationships
and even in the Church.

Everywhere I go,
negativity breeds beyond imagination.
Newspapers and television
report division, violence, lawsuits,
rape, war, scandal.
I must work hard to remember
that what you promise is not
that things will be easy,
but that you are with us,
that the pain and suffering
surrounding and consuming us
will not be the last word.

It is difficult not to be pessimistic

and see all this as naive wishful thinking.
It often seems so unattainable,
so unrealistic, so impossible.
But you challenge me to stop whining
and to work hard to communicate and live
your message of hope.

Give me strength to be positive,
to see what can lie on the other side
of all that is vile and evil.
Help me invest myself in the hope
that lies in your proclamation
and in my response. Amen.

Thursday of the First Week of Lent

Esther 12:14-16, 23-25
Psalm 138:1-2, 2-3, 7-8
Matthew 7:7-12

God,
I take so much for granted
most of the time.
I complain and groan about things
that do not go my way,
and I forget about the most simple things
given to me:
my ability to see and to walk,
the wonderful people in my life
and the fact that you have given me
another day to live.

I pray to you often,
but I don't always believe
that you answer my prayer.
I must remind myself that you respond
to my prayers,
but I do not always like
the answers you give.
I need to let go of my arrogance,
my belief that I know what is best for me,
that I know what I need most.

So often I fail to give you thanks
for your wisdom in guiding my life.
I need your grace
to help me be more thankful,
to see your goodness in all aspects of my life,
to remember that everything that happens has
   purpose
and you are the source of all blessings,
no matter how hidden you may seem to be at the
   time.

Today I will be thankful
for all that brings me both pain and joy.
I will be thankful for every person
whom I encounter today
and try to see the best in each of them,
to see your handiwork
in the essence of who they are.

Today I will seek out someone
who needs my thanks,
someone who needs to hear
a good word from me,
someone who needs to know
that he or she is good and
is a true reflection of you.

Help me breathe in nothing
but gratitude this day. Amen.

Friday of the First Week of Lent

Ezekiel 18:21-28
Psalm 130:1-2, 3-4, 4-6, 7-8
Matthew 5:20-26

God,
at times I have been taught
that anger is a bad thing,
that we should shove it
into the background at all costs,
that it is evil and wrong.

Some tell me that anger
is a good thing,
normal and healthy,
something that needs to be felt
and expressed.
We know there are times
when we *should* feel anger:
when we witness hatred,
or the death of a child,
or the loss of someone to AIDS,
or when we encounter evil.

But some people, including me,
hang on to their anger
and use it as an escape
or a way to maintain power over others.

Anger can be sneaky and seductive.
I do not always know how to channel it,
or when it is healthy,
or when it is my undoing
that can hurt others or even me.

Instead of focusing on the anger
around and within me,
I need to see through the anger—
not necessarily so I can escape it,
but so I can find your gift of peace.

Help me seek forgiveness
and shed the pride
that wants me to wear my anger
like a badge of honor.
Help me receive the honest
and courageous acts of healing from others,
from those who have hurt me.
Help me surrender my need
to be vindicated
and to let go of my pain.

Most importantly, God,
help me realize that anger is human
and a gift when it leads to peace.
Help me be an instrument of your peace. Amen.

Saturday of the First Week of Lent

Deuteronomy 26:16-19
Psalm 119:1-2, 4-5, 7-8
Matthew 5:43-48

God,
I do not understand why
I have enemies.
Some were created by my deliberate actions,
some by misunderstandings,
and some by reasons
I can no longer remember or fathom.
Some used to be close friends,
some are colleagues and coworkers,
some are even family members.
The pain that comes with having enemies
is often too much to bear:
silences, gossip about me,
ruthless behavior toward me
and sometimes a deliberate desire to hurt me.

As always, God,
you give me choices in the midst
of my hurt and pain.
You encourage me to embrace my enemies
and take my pain to a higher ground.
You do not ask me to be a doormat
that others stomp on

but to refrain from returning evil with evil.
You ask that I not haunt others or myself
with bruising pain.
You ask me simply to bless my enemies.

I need you desperately, God,
to help me to authentically greet with love
all who would harm me
and to see them the same way
I would want them to see me:
as one who is hurting,
as one whose desire to hurt others
is really a response to pain deep within.

Today I will try
to honestly wish someone well,
someone who I know
does not wish the same good for me.
I will try to look at my enemy
and see you and your goodness at work.

Help me make a wise choice
when I meet my enemy. Amen.

Second Sunday of Lent

(A) Genesis 12:1-4
  Psalm 33:4-5, 18-19, 20, 22
  2 Timothy 1:8-10
  Matthew 17:1-9

(B) Genesis 22:1-2, 9, 10-13, 15-18
  Psalm 116:10, 15, 16-17, 18-19
  Romans 8:31-34
  Mark 9:2-10

(C) Genesis 15:5-12, 17-18
  Psalm 27:1, 7-8, 8-9, 13-14
  Philippians 3:17—4:1
  Luke 9:28-36

God,
how I hate waiting!
I hate waiting in line for tickets
or to be seated at a restaurant
or when I am stuck in traffic,
waiting for a train to pass,
and I am already late for a meeting.
It drives me crazy!

You ask me to wait, too.
When I pray to you for answers,
for sickness to drift away

or for problems to be resolved,
I wait and wait for you to act.
When I need quick and decisive
answers and results,
I feel teased by this waiting,
by the brief glimpses
of your goodness and good times ahead
and solutions to my problems.

I can participate in a wonderful liturgy
or make a prayerful retreat
or experience a wonderful friendship
and bonding,
and then, snap! this good time
is over before I know it.
Then I bargain with you
for a little more good time,
and I anticipate the next happy occasion.
I am in a hurry always,
and your way seems slow to me.

Lent to me is like waiting
for a train to pass.
I'm powerless in moving the train along,
and my progress
is in someone else's hands.
During Lent you ask me
to be passionate and restless in my seeking
to return and follow you

and to change my heart.
At the same time,
you ask me to be patient,
to wait and let go of my need to control.
You ask me to hurry up, slowly.

I need your help to not give up quickly,
to see the race through,
to abide by your timeline and your method
in making yourself known to me.
I believe that the miracles
you work are timed just right
for when I need them,
not necessarily for when I want them.

Today I will enjoy your signs
and be grateful for them
instead of wondering
when the next one will come.
You will decide what I need
and when I need it.
It is truly good to be with you,
even when I am waiting. Amen.

Monday of the Second Week of Lent

Daniel 9:4-10
Psalm 79:8, 9, 11, 13
Luke 6:36-38

God,
I sometimes forget the power
that my words or behavior
can have over people in my life,
whether they be my spouse or partner,
my family and friends,
or my coworkers.
It can be easy to shame others
and to shame myself.

It is much easier—
and it certainly feels
much more powerful at the time—
to demean someone with words or judgments
than to build them up,
to show mercy to them,
or to affirm them.
We can diminish ourselves as well
because to not do so may result
in people thinking us to be arrogant.
Ironically, keeping ourselves shamed
keeps us comfortable in our self-loathing.
Then we don't have to live responsibly.

We can dwell in the darkness
of our shame and pity
and never grow and live
in your light and love.

You are compassionate, God,
and I need the power of your compassion
to melt away the sin of shaming
others and myself.
Help me to not judge others so quickly
and to live and act with tenderness
toward those with whom I live and work,
toward myself
and especially toward the stranger.

Today, God,
I plan to act differently.
I will work hard to resist my need
to knock others down.
I will try to affirm, to nurture
and to bring alive the best in everyone,
including me.
Goodness is present in all of us,
for after all, you made us.
Help me be mindful of that. Amen.

Tuesday of the Second Week of Lent

Isaiah 1:10, 16-20
Psalm 50:8-9, 16-17, 21, 23
Matthew 23:1-12

God,
you are anything but subtle
in what you ask of me.
Your words cut to the chase:
"Cease to do evil.
Learn to do good,
search for justice,
help the oppressed,
be just to the orphan,
plead for the widow."
Nothing like being direct!

On top of everything,
when I do these things,
you ask me to be subtle,
to act quietly,
to not ask for attention,
to not seek the compliments of others,
to not take credit.
You ask me to do justice
because it is the way of light,
the light that you have given
to all of us.

Help me be humble
and at the same time decisive;
to reach out;
to alleviate pain of those who suffer;
to confront homelessness,
terror and violence
that abound in our world.

Today, God,
I will do something concrete:
I will find ways
to ease the suffering of others.
I will call someone who is in need
or visit someone who is sick
or bring food to the local food pantry.
Today I will follow your word. Amen.

Wednesday of the Second Week of Lent

Jeremiah 18:18-20
Psalm 31:5-6, 14, 15-16
Matthew 20:17-28

God,
following you is hard.
I am tempted to say:
"Ask someone else."
The cost of following you is too high,
the path too risky,
the consequences too painful.

So I make two columns.
One column says if I follow you
I will know pain, ridicule, isolation,
uncertainty, conflict, death.
The other column says I will know
unending joy, peace, blessing,
fulfillment, rescue and life everlasting
if I follow you.
If only I would trust you!
How could I not choose you?
Is there an easier way?

Help me walk the walk
you have walked time and time again.
Help me drink from the same cup as you

and to trust that you will always
be with me.

Today I will try to follow you.
I will not shrink from any blows
that will come.
Today I will say to you,
"Ask me, God." Amen.

Thursday of the Second Week of Lent

Jeremiah 17:5-10
Psalm 1:1-2, 3, 4, 6
Luke 16:19-31

God,
I know that you want me to be happy.
You set me a path
to discover all that is needed
to be one with you.

To take the plunge and truly trust in you
is to be grounded in the richest soil.
To trust in you is to feel
the freshness that comes
after running in the rain
and allowing the sun to warm my heart.

You watch over me
and give me strength
to walk each day without fear
and with joy and delight.

Help me this day to be ever hopeful,
to live in the shade of your protection
and to flourish in your promise
of everlasting joy and peace.
Give me strong roots. Amen.

Friday of the Second Week of Lent

Genesis 37:3-4, 12-13, 17-28
Psalm 105:16-17, 18-19, 20-21
Matthew 21:33-43, 45-46

God,
at times this world seems
so selfish and hurtful.
It is easy to sell out
someone else for our own needs,
our own rise for power
and desire for security.

Selling out begins with our own fear
and self-loathing
and the realization that
we have not fulfilled
our expectations of ourselves.

I forget the wonder that you made me.
If I truly saw myself as part of
your tapestry, your handiwork,
I would not need to pull down someone else.
I would not need to harm others.
I would only need to recognize the gift,
the great work of art that I am.
I am part of your image.
I am part of your vision of beauty.

I am one with you.

I need healing, God,
healing from my shame
and feelings of deficiency
that fuel any desire to destroy others.

Help me release the beauty
that lies deep within me.
Help me let go of my fear
and let my light shine
and your peace fill me.

Today, God,
I will look in the mirror
and see the infinite possibilities in my life
and acknowledge your creativity
in creating me over and over again.
I will give thanks for your
unconditional love.

Open my heart
and help me see clearly. Amen.

Saturday of the Second Week of Lent

Micah 7:14-15, 18-20
Psalm 103:1-2, 3-4, 9-10, 11-12
Luke 15:1-3, 11-32

God,
your love at times
is too much to take.
I find it difficult to fathom
how you forgive me
over and over again,
without conditions
and without any diminishment
of the passionate love
you have for me.

I keep going away
and then I return to you,
and the cycle repeats itself.
I continue to dishonor
your promise and will for me,
and I keep coming back,
more sheepishly each time,
fearing that you may lock the door
to me next time.

But you keep running toward me,
arms opened,

your heart afire with a new zeal
for my possibilities.
Your eyes tell me you understand,
you accept my brokenness
and you embrace me fully.
I am wrapped in your love
and held in hope.
As you have done,
so I must do.

Today I will make the first move
and run toward one who needs my love,
my forgiveness, my admiration.
I will proclaim your love
and compassion for us.
I will set free the hurts
that I have collected over time.
I will take on new wings
and encounter in this new exchange,
a new manifestation
that you are real
and good on your word.

Thank you for not giving up on me. Amen.

Third Sunday of Lent

(A) *Exodus 17:3-17*
   Psalm 95:1-2, 6-7, 8-9
   Romans 5:1-2, 5-8
   John 4:5-42

(B) *Exodus 20:1-17*
   Psalm 19:8, 9, 10, 11
   1 Corinthians 1:22-25
   John 2:13-25

(C) *Exodus 3:1-8, 13-15*
   Psalm 103:1-2, 3-4, 6-7, 8, 11
   1 Corinthians 10:1-6, 10-12
   Luke 13:1-9

God,
no matter how hard I may try,
it is impossible
to keep anything from you.
You know every action I take,
and you can probe the most remote places
where my heart and mind
may take or tempt me.
You are everywhere;
you are in all things.
You give me numerous signs,
big and small,

to make your wisdom known to me.

Sometimes your signs are grand and dramatic,
and they speak boldly to me.
Other times your signs are just a hint,
a glimpse, a clue for me to dwell upon.
Sometimes you are the vast sea,
and sometimes you are a glass of water.
But you are there nonetheless.

Open my eyes and my heart as well
to see and hear your voice
in all my encounters and activities.
Direct me and use all the techniques
you have to reveal yourself to me.
Comfort me when I need to be comforted.
Disturb me when I need to be shaken up.
Show me your light in familiar ways
and teach me something new today
and every day.

Be there, please be there with me. Amen.

Monday of the Third Week of Lent

2 Kings 5:1-15
Psalm 42:2, 3; 43:3, 4
Luke 4:24-30

God,
it is so difficult to let go
of my need to control
the outcomes in my life,
to manipulate situations
and expectations.
My own logic and reasoning
want to explore the solutions to everything
and spoil anything beyond
my plan and my sense
of what my destiny should be.

I need to be more spontaneous, God,
to let go and surrender to the gift
of each new day that you give me.
I so desire to be free of the limits
of my schedule and calendar,
of my short- and long-range planning.

Fill me with the spontaneous gifts
of your grace,
your creativity,
your sense of humor,

and, especially, your wisdom.
Awaken me to the influences
of others who are the instruments
of your plan for me.

Today, God,
I will pay attention
to my own will and expectations—
may they not imprison me.
I will be open to and aware of
the many people and events
that reveal and illumine new light
and new possibilities.
I will transform my agenda
into the delightful dance
of options not considered before.

Help me be open to your interruptions. Amen.

Tuesday of the Third Week of Lent

Daniel 3:25, 34-43
Psalm 25:4-5, 6-7, 8-9
Matthew 18:21-35

God,
my heart can be hard at times.
I don't know why
it is so difficult to forgive.

So many times I have felt wronged,
and I want things made right.
I want the one who hurt me
to recant the vicious lies and
gossip spread about me.
I want my name cleared.
I want the other person to hurt, too,
to feel what I feel
and then to learn a lesson.

But you say I have to forgive,
not just once,
but over and over again.
Honestly, God,
it is difficult to simply forget
the wrong and the hurt
and offer my heart
in a spirit of forgiveness.

It is difficult sometimes to move on
because the pain is so intense,
and my anger has become embedded
too deep in my heart.

I want to resist you in this matter,
so I pray to you to lighten my hardened heart
and melt away my cynicism and vindictiveness
and my need to exact a pound of flesh in return.

Today, I will attempt a beginning.
I will begin at least to consider
writing a letter to someone who has harmed me
or someone who longs for my forgiveness.
I will pray to take on your spirit of compassion,
I will pray to forgive unconditionally,
as you forgive me,
time and time again.

I will try. Amen.

Wednesday of the Third Week of Lent

Deuteronomy 4:1, 5-9
Psalm 147:12-13, 15-16, 19-20
Matthew 5:17-19

God,
some laws that we are required to live by
do not seem just or equitable.
They often seem contradictory,
and do not provide
what is best for people.
Sometimes laws seem to work against
many who are powerless.

Not so with you.

Your law for me is simple and just.
Your law is my completeness,
your law is about life to the full.
While it is not easy
to walk in the light of your law,
the reward is sweetness, freedom,
grace and peace.

I need to pray to be strong
so that I will choose your law
even when it conflicts with other rules
that go against your vision

and your hope for us.

This day I will do everything I can
to live your law.
Today I will speak for those who are powerless.
Today I will be a sign of your justice.

Your law is perfect, God.
I thank you. Amen.

Thursday of the Third Week of Lent

Jeremiah 7:23-28
Psalm 95:1-2, 6-7, 8-9
Luke 11:14-23

God,
you are unique among the many gods
I have read about.
You are different from any other deity named
by those who believe in a supreme being.
You do not belittle or shame us,
or feel the need to keep us at bay.

Rather, you choose to have us close to you.
You befriend us,
you have the graciousness and generosity
to call us "God's people."
We are one with you,
and you find joy in that.
How wonderful!

Your law is simple and direct:
We will remain your people
if we cling to you as our God.
Together we will see wonders
never imagined before.

Today I will take the time

to listen to your voice
and remember that we are in this together.
Every step I take, you take with me.
And every step and movement
that you take,
you ask me to take the risk as well.

I believe in your promise.
I will try to keep mine as well. Amen.

Friday of the Third Week of Lent

Hosea 14:2-10
Psalm 81:6-8, 8-9, 10-11, 14, 17
Mark 12:28-34

God,
you call me to love you
with my entire being,
with every ounce of energy,
will and intention,
with all that I possess.
You ask me to love
in all things,
in all situations.
You ask me to love everyone I encounter.
You teach the hardest lesson:
Love my neighbor as myself.

When I look at how I fail
in loving others,
I realize that your image is correct.
When I am not the best lover to others,
I see how I love myself,
how I deprive myself of the love
you lavishly shower upon me.
Too often I reject your love
and then I show my true colors
in my dealings with others.

Help me draw upon your love, God.
Pull me closer to the wellspring
of your compassion
and care for me and for all people.
Then I will have the strength
to accept your love
and invite those with whom I live and work
to flow together down that wonderful river
of love that is you.

Today I will try to be a good lover. Amen.

Saturday of the Third Week of Lent

Hosea 6:1-6
Psalm 51:3-4, 18-19, 20-21
Luke 18:9-14

God,
how I long to know you!
I want to be close to you,
to know you well,
to become one with you,
to merge with you
fully and completely,
no holds barred.
I want to invest totally
in your heart
and in your plan for me.

While other voices
may be loud and sometimes convincing,
I long only to listen to
the song that you sing,
to feel your music deeply,
to be seduced only by your rhythm
pulsating through me.

I need courage to block out the noises
of those who want to lead me away from you.
Help me to stay the course,

to keep walking with you,
to keep you as the light
and center of my life.

Today I pray for
a new beginning,
a new opportunity
to listen and respond
to your truth,
a truth that can destroy
hatred and lies.

Help me listen well. Amen.

Fourth Sunday of Lent

(A) 1 Samuel 16:1, 6-7, 10-13
Psalm 23:1-3, 3-4, 5, 6
Ephesians 5:8-14
John 9:1-41

(B) 2 Chronicles 36:14-17, 19-23
Psalm 137:1-2, 3, 4-5, 6
Ephesians 2:4-10
John 3:14-21

(C) Joshua 5:9, 10-12
Psalm 34:2-3, 4-5, 6-7
2 Corinthians 5:17-21
Luke 15:1-3, 11-32

God,
it is easy to get tired
and to become discouraged.
I usually begin with vigor and confidence,
but then things come and beat upon me
and pound away at my enthusiasm.
My energy dries up.

But I have no choice;
I want to keep moving toward you.
I will crawl if I have to,
but I do not want to give up.

I will keep singing,
even if the tune is foreign
to everyone else.

I promise today not to forget you,
to keep you at the front and center
of everything I do.
I will call upon you
in all of my decisions,
and thank you regardless
of how things turn out,
always trying to remember
that your wisdom and hand
are in all things.

May I taste your goodness
in everything I do,
in everyone I meet
and in everyone I touch. Amen.

Monday of the Fourth Week of Lent

Isaiah 65:17-21
Psalm 30:2, 4, 5-6, 11-13
John 4:43-54

God,
it often seems as though
death and sickness conquer all,
and the weakening of our spirits
seems inevitable.
We try to run from this,
escape it and trick our way out,
but none of our strategies works.

You are always there,
offering a way out
of our own dungeon,
but we easily forget.
It is so simple, really.

Every Sunday I pray:
"Only say the word,
and I shall be healed."
I say these words,
but I do not always surrender
and let you hold me completely.
I do not fall into your arms
with complete abandon

and let you take over.

I need to remember
the fragility of my own faith,
of my own abilities,
of my own governance over those powers
that surround my life.

Guide me once more, God,
in placing all my cares before you,
in asking for your healing,
in laying at your feet
all my anxiety,
all my tears
and all my hopes.

Help me believe. Amen.

Tuesday of the Fourth Week of Lent

Ezekiel 47:1-9, 12
Psalm 46:2-3, 5-6, 8-9
John 5:1-3, 5-16

God,
in my journey to you
I find that I constantly
need to believe that you are real.
I need to believe in you
and trust that you believe in me.

Wherever your river flows,
life begins and grows
and refreshes.
The grass there is greener,
the color of the flowers more vibrant,
and your glory more astounding than ever.

You are my refuge
and strength in all things.
Everything lives from the water of life,
and my wonderful becoming
shines like the brightest sun.

With your hand in mine
I can walk roads
that have always been too rocky

and too frightening to attempt.
You have tossed me
into the river of hope,
and now I know that with you
I can accomplish great things.

You have done more than heal me.
You have taught me
how to walk again,
how to move forward,
how to embrace my life
with greater joy and enthusiasm.

How wonderful you are, God!
May I remember the waters of my own baptism.
May I remember that you have flowed
into the drought,
softened the rock and clay,
and provided a new garden of springtime.

May the waves of new life
plunge me into the fragrance
of your goodness. Amen.

Wednesday of the Fourth Week of Lent

Isaiah 49:8-15
Psalm 145:8-9, 13-14, 17-18
John 5:17-30

God,
my joy is full,
for you continually
stay close to me.
You help me to feel
safe in a way
that I have never
experienced before.

Your kindness and compassion
penetrate all the things
that plague me and keep me prisoner.
Your consolation is without condition
and always complete.
You never abandon me.
You never forget me.
You never leave me.
You are always with me.

Help me open my heart to you
and receive your presence.
Bring forth my youth again
and help the child in me

climb into your arms,
safe in the love
that only you can provide.

Awaken in me the awareness
that I do not have to climb
to the highest mountain
or journey to a far-off place to find you.
Alert me to see
that you are in my daily wanderings
and ordinary encounters,
in the eyes and faces
and the hopes and fears
of your people.

It is that simple.
You are everywhere.

Help me discover that you are very near,
and that you care for me. Amen.

Thursday of the Fourth Week of Lent

Exodus 32:7-14
Psalm 106:19-20, 21-22, 23
John 5:31-47

God,
when I ponder
the many gifts and blessings
you shower upon me,
I see continually
the image of freedom.

You offer me a way out of
or a way through
an imprisonment that suffocates:
the prison of my guilt and shame.
This shame bruises my heart,
sends me spiraling downward,
cripples me.

Feeling guilt for my wrongdoing
is not necessarily a bad thing.
Guilt can remind me that I made a mistake.
Shame, however, seduces me to believe
that I am the mistake.

You part the waters of my shame
and allow me to walk through—

or better yet, dance through—
the ruins that I have created for myself.
You bring me to a new home,
a place of welcome,
free of disaster,
a safe place.

Today I hope to remember
that my brothers and sisters
also often linger in a troubled land,
and they, too, seek peace and freedom.

May I never forget the chains
we all wear
and that your love is the key
that unlocks them. Amen.

Friday of the Fourth Week of Lent

Wisdom 2:12-22
Psalm 34:17-18, 19-20, 21, 23
John 7:1-2, 10, 25-30

God,
sometimes I think I know you,
who you are
and what you want from me.

But just when I think
I have you figured out,
you become unpredictable,
challenging me in ways
I do not expect.
You lead me to situations
and choices that seem to make no sense.
Life does not seem to be in sync
with what I believe about you.
I become confused
and put you in the position
of being unapproachable,
distant and far from my heart.

I must remind myself over and over again
that you are present in the midst
of my family and friends,
that you are present in the stranger,

and that you are concretely real,
living and breathing
in my struggles and in my tears.
In those times you almost
come from nowhere,
and then we are reunited,
and I become whole once more.

Help me, God,
unmask the disguises you wear,
and see you more clearly
and live more faithfully with you. Amen.

Saturday of the Fourth Week of Lent

Jeremiah 11:18-20
Psalm 7:2-3, 9-10, 11-12
John 7:40-53

God,
you do not haunt me
with my sinfulness,
with my failings,
with my constant stumblings
and fragile faith.

You do not repay
evil with evil,
for you are my loving link
to all that is sane and hopeful.
You are an affront
to my usual ways.
You call me to higher ground,
to be like you,
to take the risk
and live a different way,
to walk away from blindness
and live fully,
to inherit the riches
you hold for me.

I want to live justly.

I pray that you will grant me
an innocent and generous
mind and heart.

You alone are my protection,
you alone rescue me
from all who would harm me,
you alone rescue me from myself.

Today I will seek you
as my safe shelter in all things,
and I will live confidently
in the knowledge
that you will never let me go.

I trust you. Amen.

Fifth Sunday of Lent

(A) Ezekiel 37:12-14
*   Psalm 130:1-2, 3-4, 5-6, 7-8*
*   Romans 8:8-11*
*   John 11:1-45*

(B) Jeremiah 31:31-34
*   Psalm 51:3-4, 12-13, 14-15*
*   Hebrews 5:7-9*
*   John 12:20-33*

(C) Isaiah 43:16-21
*   Psalm 126:1-2, 2-3, 4-5, 6*
*   Philippians 3:8-14*
*   John 8:1-11*

God,
you are the ultimate hero
in my life.
You rescue me
from my own smell,
from my tears,
from the terror that may surround me.

You are my hero,
tender and compassionate.
You weep for me,
hurt with me

and stick with me
when everyone else runs the other way.

You are my hero,
but you also confront
and challenge me,
not allowing me to wallow
in my guilt and shame,
calling me to rise above it
and pick myself up
and walk into your light.

You are my hero,
not just once,
but over and over again,
freeing me from my prison
and celebrating my rescue.

Keep my faith strong, God,
and keep nagging at me
to move beyond my dying
to embrace the surprise
of your light. Amen.

Monday of the Fifth Week of Lent

Daniel 13:1-9, 15-17, 19-30, 33-62
Psalm 23:1-3, 3-4, 5, 6
(A, B) John 8:1-11; (C) John 8:12-20

God,
I need your guiding hand today.

I so desperately want
to walk the right path
and allow you
to lead me to all the right places,
to make all the right choices.
I want to say the right word,
give the right look
and be the best I can be
for my work, my friends
and those who are important to me.

You have prepared the way
and set me upon it safely.
You are always there
when I call upon you.
You steady me
when I feel fearful.

Help me know
that you desire only good for me,

that your wish is that I dwell
in happiness always.

I intend to set forth from this place
to follow your way
and trust that you
will never lead me into
a hole too deep to climb out of.

I will hold quietly the belief
that you are here with me always. Amen.

Tuesday of the Fifth Week of Lent

Numbers 21:4-9
Psalm 102:2-3, 16-18, 19-21
John 8:21-30

God,
I feel shaky,
uncertain and afraid,
and sometimes I do not know why.

I despise my fearfulness,
and I hate how it can sabotage
so many possibilities for me.
It can paralyze me
and make me terribly anxious.
I feel vulnerable
and terrified that I will be
eaten alive by it all.

Hear my prayer, God,
and help me to reach and find you.
Do not hide from me.
Answer my fear
with the peace I know
you can instill in me.

I need your strength more than ever.
Silence my groaning.

Cast out demons that suffocate me
and hold my insides in a choking grip.

Calm me, hold me,
whisper gently words of assurance:
"I will never leave you."

I believe that in you,
I can find peace. Amen.

Wednesday of the Fifth Week of Lent

Daniel 3:14-20, 91-92, 95
Daniel 3:52-56
John 8:31-42

God,
everything around me seems so busy.
Everything feels frantic and harried.
Now you give me Lent,
this wonderful time to slow down,
to be still,
to reflect.

This silent time is scary
because it is the time when
I hear you more clearly,
and I do not always
like what I hear.
You challenge me
because you know everything about me.
You know my thoughts
and my fears
and the secrets I hide from everyone else
and sometimes, even from myself.
You scare me
when you reach deep within my heart
and embrace the darkest
and most painful things

that I do not want to face
and that bury me in shame.

I do not know how to handle your love.
It is too much,
too unconditionally accepting
and too hopeful of a change in me.
It is easier for me to keep busy,
to let my complicated calendar
and frantic activity shield me
from the most intimate part of myself:
the place where you see me
as my truest self.

I need you, God,
to help me stop and face the stillness.
Help me conquer my fear
of walking the long hallway
of my heart and soul,
of seeing what you see,
of accepting with love and compassion
what I loathe and despise in myself.

You do not abandon me,
so why should I?

Help me to be alone with myself,
and be at peace with it all
and enjoy myself. Amen.

Thursday of the Fifth Week of Lent

Genesis 17:3-9
Psalm 105:4-5, 6-7, 8-9
John 8:51-59

God,
you are the source
of all that is good in my life.
You are the beginning
and end of all creation and history.
You are all that is within,
all that is before me,
above and below.

Because of your magnificent love for me,
I, too, am able to share
in the fullness of your glory
and am invited to become one with you
in the celebration of life.

Give me the openness I need
to receive you.
Loosen my hands when they are tightly closed.
Help me stretch my arms wide
to let your glory refresh me.

In all my actions,
may I be attentive and present

to those in need.
May I listen well
and accept lovingly with an open heart
the journey that you ask me to take
with my brothers and sisters.

You are my past,
my present
and my future.

You are all I need.
Help me to remember. Amen.

Friday of the Fifth Week of Lent

Jeremiah 20:10-13
Psalm 18:2-3, 3-4, 5-6, 7
John 10:31-42

God,
when I am close to you
I feel strong.
With you at my side,
I find much to feast upon.

You are my help.
When the waves of death rise
about me from every side,
I cry to you and you listen.
You are relentless in not giving up on me.
You believe in me.

Your words become my lifeline,
and your cross helps me realize
that holiness is not pious fantasy
but my destiny.

The life you give me
redefines what it means
to breathe, to see,
to hear, to touch,
to cry, to laugh,

to experience pain and suffering
and the gift that it holds for me.

I want to celebrate the understanding
that your will for me
is to live—totally.

Thank you for my life,
all of it. Amen.

Saturday of the Fifth Week of Lent

Ezekiel 37:21-28
Jeremiah 31:10, 11-12, 13
John 11:45-57

God,
it is so easy to be negative
and ridicule those who try to do good.

I am tempted to tear down,
to bring others to their knees,
to put them in their place
with my sharp tongue.
I can be quick to burst
their bubble,
shatter their joy
and squash a wonderful moment
just as it begins to rise.
I feel powerful in this ability.

But you confront me
and make it all too clear
that when I act this way,
I am really angry with myself
or filled with my own disgust
and disappointment.

You ask us to delight in one another,

to nurture each other
and to breathe your passion
for goodness and light
in all people.
We all are your creation,
your works of art,
and I forget that.
I am sorry.

Today I want to change.
Today I want to contradict
the conventional wisdom
that I must break someone else
in order to feel confident and competent.
You are all I need to feel secure.
I do not need to cheapen your vision
by robbing others of their dignity.
I will be positive.
I will revel with someone else
when they celebrate a victory.
I will share in others' joy
and delight in your action
in our lives. Amen.

Passion Sunday (Palm Sunday)

Isaiah 50:4-7
Psalm 22:8-9, 17-18, 19-20, 23-24
Philippians 2:6-11
(A) Matthew 26:14—27:66;
    (B) Mark 14:1—15:47; (C) Luke 22:14—23:56

God,
I am tempted strongly
to short-cut
the trip you want me
to take with you.

You want me to bring my own story
into communion with yours.
You want me to enter this chapter with joy,
knowing full well
that rejection and pain
lie not far away.

I wish I could skip Lent
and jump directly into Easter
and not have to face
the painful part of your story.

Take my hand today, God,
and help me to be strong,
to listen well

and to be present to all that lies ahead this week.

May I take up your cross today
and take on your suffering
that will lead me beyond the grave
and into the everlasting joy of your arms.

Blessed is the one
who comes in your name,
and blessed am I
when I journey with you. Amen.

Monday of Holy Week

Isaiah 42:1-7
Psalm 27:1, 2, 3, 13-14
John 12:1-11

God,
sometimes everything pounds on me,
and the pressure is too much.
My stomach tightens,
my chest hurts
and I feel like I cannot breathe.

I need you to help me manage
all that makes me anxious.
I need you to help me calm down
and find a space of sanity
before I tumble again into
this terrifying cycle.

I know you can help me
because you are the source
of all that lives and grows,
and you can create me new again.
You can bring me breath and freshness.
You can take me into your hand,
form me again, reshape my vision,
pull me from darkness.

Now is when I hold you
to your word:
that you are my God,
that you care,
that you will save me.

I will sing to you today:
You are my light
and my salvation.
Why should I fear?

I will wait for you always. Amen.

Tuesday of Holy Week

Isaiah 49:1-6
Psalm 71:1-2, 3-4, 5-6, 15, 17
John 13:21-33, 36-38

God,
I work so hard and so many hours
on some projects,
and still it seems as though
nothing gets done.
Often when a project is finished,
and I have broken my back
and sweated over details
to meet a deadline,
the reward seems almost nonexistent.

I am sure you feel the same way at times;
at least I would understand if you did.
You give me every opportunity to choose well,
to live in fidelity to you
and to live justly.
And whatever you get from me in return
usually falls short.

You are my strength, God,
and you challenge me to consider
that living in communion
with you is reward enough.

With you and in your sight
I am the best creation possible,
a reflection of you.

May I always thank you and praise you
for your generosity.
May I sing and dance with abandon,
knowing that to walk with you
is to move toward paradise.

You are all I need. Amen.

Wednesday of Holy Week

Isaiah 50:4-9
Psalm 69:8-10, 21-22, 31, 33-34
Matthew 26:14-25

God,
you never allow me
to sit comfortably,
to relax and be passive.
Every day, relentlessly,
you choose to open a door
within my heart and speak to me.
Even if I should desire it,
I cannot block out your voice.

When I am at my best,
I do not shrink from you.
I try to respond in faith,
with joy and with assurance
that you will not bring me harm
and that you have chosen me
to be your presence,
to be your voice for those who choose to listen.

Today I ask you again
to give me the courage
to be my best self,
to summon all my gifts,

all my desire
and all my love
to let you in
and allow your grace
to move where it will.

You ask me to give over
everything to you.
I hope to make you proud this day. Amen.

Holy Thursday

Exodus 12:1-8, 11-14
Psalm 116:12-13, 15-16, 17-18
1 Corinthians 11:23-26
John 13:1-15

God,
today begins Triduum,
this special three days
when you ask me
and all those who believe in you
to glory in the cross.

How can we revel in the cross,
the very instrument
that brings death and humiliation?

You ask me to stop and consider.
You ask me to follow your example
of pain and suffering.
You ask me to be broken
and to pour myself out.
You ask me to pay the price
as you did
to purify the struggles and dyings
of all of us.

No greater love exists

than for us to lay down our life,
to keep alive
the vision of new life
that you have so wonderfully
promised us.

As you have done, so I must do. Amen.

Good Friday

Isaiah 52:13-53, 12
Psalm 31:2, 6, 12-13, 15-16, 17, 25
Hebrews 4:14-16; 5:7-9
John 18:1-19, 42

God,
today I celebrate the incredible realization
that you have not abandoned me.

You continually restore my hope
and never tire in your passion for me,
even in the midst
of this most unquestionable horror story:
the agony of blood and nails and thorns,
the loneliness of the cross,
the abandonment by friends and followers.

You ask me to travel to the dark place as well
and feel your searing pain,
feel your loneliness,
feel your grief of disloyalty.

Come to me today
and sign me with your cross.
May I wear the cross proudly
and always live as your servant.
Into your hands, God, I commend my life. Amen.

Easter Vigil

Genesis 1:1-2; 2
Psalm 104:1-2, 5-6, 10, 12, 13-14, 24, 35;
*   or Psalm 33:4-5, 6-7, 12-13, 20-22*
Genesis 22:1-18
Psalm 16:5, 8, 9-10, 11
Exodus 14:15—15:1
Exodus 15:1-2, 3-4, 5-6, 17-18
Isaiah 54:5-14
Psalm 30:2, 4, 5-6, 11-12, 13
Isaiah 55:1-11
Isaiah 12:2-3, 4, 5 6
Baruch 3:9-15, 32—4:4
Psalm 19:8, 9, 10, 11
Ezekiel 36:16-28
Psalm 42:3, 5; 43:3, 4
Romans 6:3-11
Psalm 118:1-2, 16, 17, 22-23
(A) Matthew 28:1-10; (B) Mark 16:1-8;
*   (C) Luke 24:1-12*

God,
I come to you
awed by your loving power
in my life.

I feel your fire—
the warm spark of your love

and the roaring blaze
that can destroy
all that is obsessed with death,
all that is poisoned by hate,
all that rapes the earth,
all that nurtures despair.

I hear your word,
your story that is my story as well—
a story that you ask me to remember
and tell over and over again,
a story in which you promise
the most glorious of happy endings,
a story that defies
our expectations of this life.

Hope is not a fantasy!
Death will not win!
Justice and peace will embrace!
The stench of the tomb is replaced
with the wonderful sweetness
of your heavenly dwelling!

How I desire to be drenched
in the purifying waters of Baptism!
How I desire to be immersed
in your life-giving waters,
in all that is growing,
in all that cleanses and refreshes

and creates a new masterpiece
within me!

You anoint me with your love,
its deep and strong fragrance
impossible to wash off;
your anointing oil glistens and drips
and finds its way
to every corner of my spirit.

But the greatest honor of all
is your invitation
to come and sit at your table
and share in the delicious
feast of love and sustenance
that you have prepared especially
for your family.
That's us!
You humble and honor me
with this meal
and the many meals to come.

I thank you and praise you
for this wonderful journey
that celebrates all that I am,
all that you are
and all that awaits me
throughout my life with you. Amen.

Easter Sunday

Acts 10:34, 37-43
Psalm 118:1-2, 16-17, 22-23
Colossians 3:1-4 or 1 Corinthians 5:6-8
John 20:1-9

God,
you are truly amazing.

You give more than a miracle to observe:
You proclaim a story to be more
than a remembrance of history.
The victory of Jesus is our victory as well!
Alleluia!

I, too, share in these new possibilities—
that hope is real,
that new life is not a mirage,
that your love for us is stronger
and more powerful
than any other.
Alleluia!

You call me to witness
not just about Jesus in the Scriptures,
Jesus who has died and is risen,
but about Jesus who is here,
now and forever.

Jesus is alive,
moving and breathing in us,
and rolling away the stone from our tombs,
not just once,
but over and over again,
with new strength each time.
This is my song today:
Because of Jesus
my sins are forgiven.
Alleluia!

The stone is gone from the entrance to my heart.
Jesus has entered my life
and unlocked all that lay in darkness.
The wrappings of death and sin are left behind,
and now I am clothed with the joy of new life!
Alleluia!

May I bear witness to this new life
in all that I encounter today. Amen. Alleluia!

Monday of the Octave of Easter

Acts 2:14, 22-32
Psalm 16:1-2, 5, 7-8, 9-10, 11
Matthew 28:8-15

God,
I praise and thank you
for your gift of new life,
for your message of hope
that flows constantly
from your presence.

Resurrection is hard to accept.
Like the women at the tomb,
I am overjoyed yet fearful.
I recognize that your rising
forces me to look forward,
to not get lost looking back
at darkness and hopelessness.
It is much easier, sometimes,
much more seductive
and less complicated,
to live as I lived before your rising:
half-alive in a tomb.

New life means new challenges,
new paths to journey,
new ways of looking at things.

With your Resurrection,
I am called to live my life differently.

You call me to convert my life,
to proclaim the good news of salvation
not just with my words
but with my entire life.
This good news is difficult to carry
because proclaiming it will not wipe away
suffering or destroy death.
Today I hear the words
"Peace" and "Do not be afraid."
But many are afraid.
I am afraid.

It is easy to desire a resurrection
that delivers remedies and quick solutions
to the terrors of life.
But that is not your way.
The promise you make to me
and to all of us
is that we will not be alone.
You promise to be with me.
Always.
No matter what.
That is enough for me.

Help me trust in this promise
and help others trust in it as well. Amen.

Tuesday of the Octave of Easter

Acts 2:36-41
Psalm 33:4-5, 18-19, 20, 22
John 20:11-18

God,
everywhere I look
and in everyone whom I love
I see the fullness of your goodness.

You alone I trust.
In you I find true justice.
In you I witness a kindness
I have never experienced.
You continue to rise within me
and point me to new directions.
You open new doors
that lead to exciting
and wonderful places.

You melt the barriers of my heart
and call me to conversion.
May I always be open to you
and realize that every day
you call me to be born again.

I call out to you, God:
Come to me

and renew me
with the wonderful life you provide
when I listen to you,
when I share your presence with others
and when I truly see you.

My eyes long to gaze upon you,
not an image of you
or some artist's rendering.
I want to see you
in my family and friends
and in the eyes and lives
of all my brothers and sisters.

Thank you for revealing yourself to me:
"I have seen the Lord!"
You know me well,
and I long to know you better.

I have seen you.
May I never lose sight of you. Amen.

Wednesday of the Octave of Easter

Acts 3:1-10
Psalm 105:1-2, 3-4, 6-7, 8-9
Luke 24:13-35

God,
you are so wonderful
because you choose us
to share in your glory!
Such a wonderful gift!

You help me to see your wonderful work
in the most simple and ordinary things.
It is easy to get wrapped up
in incredible events,
to look for miracles and apparitions
and extraordinary visions.
The miracles you give are subtle
and yet powerful.
What you ask of me
is not to effect dramatic changes
and events that will help people,
but to be attentive and present
to those in need.

What I can do
is use my eyes,
my voice, my ears

to witness others' pain and suffering
and hold them close to my heart
as you did.
As you still do now.

You simply ask me to welcome others,
share my story,
listen to their stories,
and be open to how you become known
in the most ordinary relationships
and in the most simple gatherings.

Help me to stay focused,
to be present. Amen.

Thursday of the Octave of Easter

Acts 3:11-26
Psalm 8:2, 5, 6-7, 8-9
Luke 24:35-48

God,
like your disciples
in the joy of resurrection,
I, too, can easily forget
what cost you paid for our salvation.

Even though I have suffered many times
and even though you continually save me,
I never seem to fully grasp
what life in you means.
It means suffering,
it means taking up the cross,
it means that in being broken
we can be put back together again.

I must remember that you have made me
little less than you,
for what other reason would there be
for me to receive your glory?
I certainly do not deserve your love,
but you constantly reward me
and crown me with your goodness.
I must remember that I can only receive this

because of your ultimate sacrifice.

You ask the same of me.
You ask me to walk the road that Jesus walked.
You ask me to bear the blows he received.
You ask me to wear the crown of pain
that he wore.
On my road to Calvary
you will be with me.
On my road to resurrection
you will be with me.

We will be one.
Together. Always.
Glory to you, God. Amen.

Friday of the Octave of Easter

Acts 4:1-12
Psalm 118:1-2, 4, 22-24, 25-27
John 21:1-14

God,
with you I can accomplish
great things!

You lavishly forgive,
you give us each day
as a new possibility,
a new chance,
a new beginning!

Blessed am I
when I live your way,
when I speak in your name,
when I serve you.

You are the cornerstone of my life,
the foundation for all my efforts.
You never abandon me
nor leave me for dead.
With you, great things are possible!

I do not need to look anywhere else,
I do not need to cry out to agencies

and organizations,
I do not need self-help books
or medication or therapy
to be saved.
Only you can save.
Only you can enlighten my heart.
Only you can help me believe in myself.
Only you can help me surmount
whatever obstacles come my way.
Only you.
Only you.

Help me remember
that you are all that I need. Amen.

Saturday of the Octave of Easter

Acts 4:13-21
Psalm 118:1, 14-15, 16-18, 19-21
Mark 16:9-15

God,
you are truly amazing!

I wonder sometimes
about who you choose
to be your witnesses.
I do not understand why
you choose certain people,
myself included,
to be your messengers,
to be your vessels.

To be blunt:
I don't feel qualified!
You know my flaws,
you know my sins,
you know how I mess up
over and over again.

Yet, you choose me,
and because of that,
some people find it difficult
to believe that you could be working

through me and in me.

I need your help to endure ridicule
when I act in your name.
I need your presence
when I lack courage and want
someone else to do your work.
You will not let me off the hook,
I know.
So stay with me.
Don't give up on me.
Pick me up when I fall.
Keep loving me as you always have.

Rise in me,
and be my strength and courage
in all things. Amen.

Second Sunday of Easter

(A) Acts 2:42-47
  Psalm 118:2-4, 13-15, 22-24
  1 Peter 1:3-9
  John 20:19-31

(B) Acts 4:32-35
  Psalm 118:2-4, 13-15, 22-24
  1 John 5:1-6
  John 20:19-31

(C) Acts 5:12-16
  Psalm 118:2-4, 13-15, 22-24
  Revelation 1:9-11, 12-13, 17-19
  John 20:19-31

God,
with you by our side,
we can do marvelous things!

Like the first disciples,
you call all of us
to follow you.

You ask us to share
everything we have,
to look for those in need
and respond with generosity.

Everywhere we look, it seems,
people hoard and hold onto
what is closest to them.
We look the other way
when what we see makes us uncomfortable.
Why are there so many who need
and so few who respond?

You ask us to build your Church,
the body whom you call your own.
It is difficult to grasp your vision
when it clashes with the values
that surround us.

You ask us to pray daily.
Why is it so difficult sometimes
just to get to church on Sunday?

You ask us to be of one heart and one mind
and treat others with reverence,
respect and honor;
to heal and reach out to each other,
to be attentive,
to put the needs and concerns of others
ahead of our own.

What you ask does not mirror our experience.
What you ask is foreign
to how we live our life,

to the way we behave,
even when we come together in church.

God,
during this time of Easter,
open my eyes to the needs around me.
Convert me to a life
that is more than lip-service,
more than appearances,
more than good intentions and lovely thoughts.
I need to act and to challenge
my brothers and sisters to act, too.

May the acts of the Apostles
be the playbook by which I approach
my life and my faith. Amen.

Monday of the Second Week of Easter

Acts 4:23-31
Psalm 2:1-3, 4-6, 7-9
John 3:1-8

God,
you are wonderful indeed!
The signs and wonders
around me can come only from you.

Your signs and wonders
are everywhere when I am open
to seeing and experiencing them.

I need to remember
that your gifts and miracles
can be found every day
in the ordinary, subtle
and sometimes hidden things of life.
It is easy to want to see
something impressive,
something dramatic,
something absolutely extraordinary.

But Easter tells me
that your wonder exists
in the most obvious
and in what I take for granted.

I am awed sometimes
that I awake each morning,
that I can do simple tasks,
that I can walk,
that I can sing,
that I can see.

The most awesome thing
I know is that
you never give up on me.
You are tireless in reaching out to me.
You are relentless in your faith in me,
even when I lose faith in myself.

Thank you for your love
that brings me new life. Amen.

Tuesday of the Second Week of Easter

Acts 4:32-37
Psalm 93:1-2, 5
John 3:7-15

God,
I find it difficult
and frustrating at times
to know you.
You are unpredictable,
uncontrollable
and yet so wonderful.

Sometimes I feel as though
I know where I am headed.
My path seems clear,
and I think I can coast through life.
I like having things figured out,
having my agenda clear,
feeling in control of my days.

And then you decide
with your wonderful sense of humor
(I hope that's what it is)
to throw a diversion my way,
to mix things up a bit,
and, to be honest, complicate things.

This drives me crazy
because it interrupts the flow of my life
and causes me great stress.
I become anxious and angry
because you are getting in the way
of my plans.

But your spirit blows where it wills,
certainly not where I want it to go.
I need to remember that the interruption
in the midst of my particular agenda
is now the agenda.
I need to see that
your way is better for me.

Help me let go of my need to control
and accept what you have in store for me.
Lead me. Amen.

Wednesday of the Second Week of Easter

Acts 5:17-26
Psalm 34:2-3, 4-5, 6-7, 8-9
John 3:16-21

God,
I praise you
because I know
that you are always with me.

I forget that you carry me through rough times
and lead me out of the darkness.

I am totally amazed that you love me,
totally in awe that you gave us your Son.
I am amazed that all you ask in return
is that we believe and live in your light.

It should be easy to live in the light.
But why is it, even when my intentions are good,
I choose the wrong way?
Why do I continually make choices
that don't agree with your plan for me?
I am dumbfounded to know
that you do not lose patience with me,
get exasperated with me
or love me any less.

Help me to see only light,
to not only hear the truth,
but to become your truth,
to live your way
and in your promise. Amen.

Thursday of the Second Week of Easter

Acts 5:27-33
Psalm 34:2, 9, 17-18, 19-20
John 3:31-36

God,
it is you I seek,
it is you I want to follow
all the days of my life.

I need your strength this day, God.
I need to listen to your voice
and hear your direction for me
when other voices vie to control me
and lead me their way.

The voices are many:
I hear them at work,
among my family and friends and foes.
The voices distract me
and are loud and seductive.
I am drawn to these voices
that lead me into trouble.

God,
your voice is quiet.
Even your silence
speaks to me.

You want me to choose,
you do not force me.
You give me free will
and the responsibility
to choose my own destiny.

Help me, God,
to believe in you alone,
to trust that you will never lead me
into danger,
that you want the best for me.

The destination you hold out to me
is better than any place
I have traveled to:
eternal life.

Help my unbelief. Amen.

Friday of the Second Week of Easter

Acts 5:34-42
Psalm 27:1, 4, 13-14
John 6:1-15

G<small>od</small>,
you alone are enough.
I need nothing more.

At times I think I need so many things:
more possessions,
more money,
more friends,
more affirmation,
more, more, more!

I know I am not alone in this need.
Everybody wants to be fed by you,
everybody has needs,
everybody wants more,
everybody wants you to give them what they
   want—
financial security,
stability in their families,
fulfillment in their love lives,
more success in their jobs
and more assurances of your presence.

Help all of us to remember
that we have enough,
that you have multiplied
your love for us
more than we can possibly hope for.
You have time and time again
given us the gift of you,
always with us,
always forgiving,
always faithful,
always trusting,
always there
and always here.

Your love is always left over
to nourish us even more.

Help me remember
that you give me all that I need
and that you call me to give all that I have,
whatever that may be,
and that will be enough. Amen.

Saturday of the Second Week of Easter

Acts 6:1-7
Psalm 33:1-2, 4-5, 18-19
John 6:16-21

God,
thank you for the gift
of new life,
of new beginnings,
and the power that is given to us
if only we believe.

Honestly, God,
it can get a bit tiresome,
surviving and getting through one crisis
only to realize that another one awaits.
When it rains, it pours!
The storms sometimes never seem to stop;
they don't let up
or give me a chance to breathe
and enjoy the sunshine for a while.

Ridiculously, I think I can on my own power
rise above any trial, somehow fix it
and claim victory over it.

Yet my boat still sinks!
Why can't I remember that only you

can walk across the abyss
and reach out to me?
Only you can calm the waters
that thrash within my soul.

Help me, God,
to offer my fear to you
and rest securely in knowing
that you are with me always. Amen.

Third Sunday of Easter

(A) Acts 2:14, 22-28
Psalm 16:1-2, 5, 7-8, 9-10, 11
1 Peter 1:17-21
Luke 24:13-35

(B) Acts 3:13-15, 17-19
Psalm 4:2, 4, 7-8, 9
1 John 2:1-5
Luke 24:35-48

(C) Acts 5:27-32, 40-41
Psalm 30:2, 4, 5-6, 11-12, 13
Revelation 5:11-14
John 21:1-19

G od,
how I love you!

Your actions in my life
are far too many to mention,
too wonderful to fathom
and more powerful than anything in the world.
Your Resurrection is more than theatrics,
more than exciting drama,
more than amazing feats and wonders!

You continually rise in me,

prodding me with questions and challenges:
"What are you discussing?"
"Did not the Messiah have to undergo all this?"
"Why are you disturbed?"
"Children, have you nothing to eat?"
And most troubling of all:
"Do you love me?"

Answering these questions makes me
tongue-tied and terribly nervous.
How can I possibly answer you properly?
How can I present an answer
that you do not already know?

You know I love you.
And because you know,
you raise the stakes,
asking me to share the Good News,
offer witness with my story
and feed your sheep.

Help me love you more
each and every day. Amen.

Monday of the Third Week of Easter

Acts 6:8-15
Psalm 119:23-24, 26-27, 29-30
John 6:22-29

God,
I praise you.
You have searched me
and probed my heart
and rescued me from myself.

I sometimes am impressed with myself,
proud of how I try to live
and proud of just how well
I live out my faith.

But you know
(of course you know),
that I live comfortably,
that I suffer no outward persecution for my faith,
that I live in a country and society
that calls itself Christian,
that I experience no discrimination or abuse
because of my faith and belief in you.

Would I be willing to die for you?
Would I be courageous and trusting enough
in my faith to make the ultimate sacrifice?

Would I deny you if my life depended on it?
Which life am I talking about—
the life I find comfort in
or the life that you want for me?
How would I answer?
To be honest, I don't know.

All I know is that I need you
to strengthen me and give me courage
to face all the tests that come my way,
to reject the voices and actions
that bar me from being close to you.

Be with me. Amen.

Tuesday of the Third Week of Easter

Acts 7:51—8:1
Psalm 31:3-4, 6, 7, 8, 17, 21
John 6:30-35

God,
all goodness and light come from you.
All wondrous gifts I receive come from you.

I sometimes forget that.
When good things come my way,
I thank so many—
my friends and family,
my intuition and insight,
my own genius.
Then, when something horrible happens,
when the bottom falls out and my genius fails me
and no solutions appear,
I call on you, God, my last resort.
I should consider you
my first strategy for undoing havoc,
my first source for problem-solving,
my first choice for finding peace.

You are in everything.
You are sanity amid insanity.
You are the source of all good things.
All that is good in my life comes from you,

and all that lifts me up is from you.

Help me remember
that you are with me all the time.
Help me call upon you in my life
when things are great
and when things are not so great.

Give me the insight to know
that you belong at the center of my life. Amen.

Wednesday of the Third Week of Easter

Acts 8:1-8
Psalm 66:1-3, 4-5, 6-7
John 6:35-40

God,
it is amazing
that once people find out about you—
the real you—
you captivate them!
Day after day, event after event,
you make yourself known to me:
when I experience the beauty
and wonder about me
and when I experience you in my aloneness,
my pain and my despair.

When word gets out about you,
when we see that all blessings come from you,
we change and see things differently
and are never the same.

You ask me to go outside my comfort zone,
outside of what is known
and share what I know to be true:
that you are God
and there is no other like you.

Thank you for the honor to serve you,
to share with others the joy
that is so tremendous
it has calmed the chaotic sea of my life
and helped me cross over to dry land.

May I sing joyfully to you
and proclaim my praise
to the ends of the earth. Amen.

Thursday of the Third Week of Easter

Acts 8:26-40
Psalm 66:8-9, 16-17, 20
John 6:44-51

God,
with you I can live forever!

Of course,
I know that this does not mean
that I will not die someday;
I know I will.
What I am learning more and more from you
is that eternal life means
that my physical death will not be the end
but the entrance into a new way of being.

I should not fear death, but I do.
Your Resurrection means that
while I will still experience death and suffering,
it will not win out over me,
it will not consume me,
it will not destroy my hope.

You are my hope.
You are the bread that can satisfy me.
You invite me to dine with you
and experience a meal

that is the finest cuisine of all—
relationship with you.

When we meet each other,
when we intimately connect,
I am whole.

I believe in you, God.
Strengthen me in my belief. Amen.

Friday of the Third Week of Easter

Acts 9:1-20
Psalm 117:1, 2
John 6:52-59

God,
your power is absolutely unbelievable!
You can move the biggest mountains,
and you can melt the hardest of hearts.

It is difficult for me to accept
that people can change,
especially those who cause harm,
who seem full of themselves,
who delight in walking a darker path.
When someone like that begins acting differently,
I become suspicious and question the motive.
Why the sudden change?

Then I realize how judgmental I have become.
I should remember that I am not perfect myself.
There is much of which I am not proud
and for which I feel shame.

You turned my heart around, didn't you?
You gave me another chance, didn't you?
They deserve the same chance, don't they?
They, too, are capable of conversion, aren't they?

You see the potential in me, over and over again,
don't you?

God, open my heart to recognize
that with you anything is possible
and anybody can change,
that everyone is loved by you. Amen.

Saturday of the Third Week of Easter

Acts 9:31-42
Psalm 116:12-13, 14-15, 16-17
John 6:60-69

God,
it is absolutely impossible
to adequately pay you back
for all that you give to me.
How can I possibly thank you?
How can I possibly do anything
to measure up to your mercy and kindness,
to your glory?

You ask me to perform "miracles"—
not dramatic miracles like turning
water into wine
or parting a body of water,
but rather the miracle of listening to someone
who is hurting;
the miracle of walking with someone
who is lonely;
the miracle of giving to someone in need.

I cannot be you.
I just have to be the best me possible.
Help me remain true
to the gift of your life. Amen.

Fourth Sunday of Easter

(A) *Acts 2:14, 36-41*
   Psalm 23:1-3, 3-4, 5, 6
   1 Peter 2:20-25
   John 10:1-10

(B) *Acts 4:8-12*
   Psalm 118:1, 8-9, 21-23, 26, 21, 29
   1 John 3:1-2
   John 10:11-18

(C) *Acts 13:14, 43-52*
   Psalm 100:1-2, 3, 5
   Revelation 7:9, 14-17
   John 10:27-30

God,
to be given the name "child of God"
is an honor like no other!

You humble me with the regard you hold for me,
and you give me new wings to fly.
Like you, I rise and move
like a mighty wind
and soar like the eagle.

Thank you for the many ways
that you shepherd and guide me;

for the many ways
that you keep me close to you,
ever in your care.

You continually open new doors for me,
and when I feel frightened,
you take me by the hand and lead me safely
to the other side.
You pull me beyond the shame of myself
and make me more than acceptable.
Through your suffering, pain and death,
you took on my guilt and you rose for me,
for me!

Because of your wounds, I am healed,
no longer an outcast,
now a member of your sheepfold.
You are my guardian.

You, God, are my shepherd.
May I dwell in your house
all the days of my life. Amen.

Monday of the Fourth Week of Easter

> *Acts 11:1-18*
> *Psalm 42:2-3; 43:3, 4*
> *John 10:1-10; (A) John 10:11-18*

God,
you love everyone,
no matter who they are,
no matter where they come from,
no matter what they are like!

It is hard for me to accept everyone.
I do not like some people
because of the way they act,
the things they do,
the way they treat others.
Even their mannerisms, gestures and habits
annoy me.

It amazes me that you accept everyone,
that all have a claim to your promises,
that all are welcome at your table.
You show no partiality, thank goodness.
Your voice can be heard by everyone,
and anyone can enter your Reign.

Help me and everyone, God,
to thirst for you. Amen.

Tuesday of the Fourth Week of Easter

Acts 11:19-26
Psalm 87:1-3, 4-5, 6-7
John 10:22-30

God,
thank you for knowing me so well.

I desperately need to have someone in my life
with whom I can be totally myself,
someone with whom I don't have to play games.
I am totally vulnerable to you.
I am both grateful—and spooked—
to know that you know
what I am thinking,
what I am feeling
without me even having to speak.

I hear your voice,
and you hear my voice
hidden in the hallways
of my heart and soul.
You know me fully,
and you make yourself
known to me.

Keep your voice loud and clear, God.
I promise to listen well. Amen.

Wednesday of the Fourth Week of Easter

Acts 12:24—13:5
Psalm 67:2-3, 5, 6, 8
John 12:44-50

God,
you are life everlasting!
You are my faith,
you are my life and glory,
my happiness.
You fill my bowl to the brim.

Wherever you are,
things change, things grow,
and life sprouts everywhere!

When you enter my heart,
you invite me to something new,
something meaningful,
something that causes me
to never want to look back.

I believe in you,
and I hope that you will
always believe in me.
With you I can see,
with you I can be happy,
with you I can breathe

the freshness of the most gentle breeze,
that is you.

You do not condemn me;
you shower me with your light;
and you look on me,
seeing in me Christ within.

I do not always see it,
but you do.
You see the best in me,
you see the power
that comes from you alone,
and you ask me
to say yes to you.

Help me always say yes to you. Amen.

Thursday of the Fourth Week of Easter

Acts 13:13-25
Psalm 89:2-3, 21-22, 25, 27
John 13:16-20

God,
the joy that is possible through you
is beyond anything I have ever known.

Thank you for embracing my humanity,
for clothing me with a dignity I do not deserve.
I need you to keep loving me.
I need you to sustain me
as I try to live "new life" in all that I do.

Help me, God,
to accept the mystery of your rising,
so that I may sing forever of your love,
and know with utmost assurance,
that you exist, that you care
and that my life has meaning.

Help me be faithful
and wear with pride
your mercy and forgiveness,
so I, too, can rise again. Amen.

Friday of the Fourth Week of Easter

Acts 13:26-33
Psalm 2:6-7, 8-9, 10-11
John 14:1-6

God,
you uphold me,
you are my life.

I need you to hear me
like you always have,
for I can so easily lose heart,
become cynical
and come to think
that rising from the dead
is just pious optimism.

I need to have faith again,
something to believe in,
because at times
everything around me
seems to be falling apart.

You encourage me to not be troubled,
to have faith in you
and to believe that you have a place for me.
I need to hold you to that
because sometimes that is all I have.

I am counting on you, God,
to clear the way for me,
to prepare a place where my fears
will be acknowledged
and loved into new hope.

I do not know where you are going,
and I need you to be the way for me.

Make the path visible,
and guide my steps.
Then I will be safe.
With you. Amen.

Saturday of the Fourth Week of Easter

Acts 13:44-52
Psalm 98:1, 2-3, 3-4
John 14:7-14

God,
you hold for me a destiny
that is greater than any treasure
I could imagine.

How I long to see you,
just once,
to get a glimpse of what you are really like—
and to figure out your methods, your ways
and the "transactions" you make with me.
You seem to keep yourself hidden,
you seem so unknowable,
so full of mystery,
so full of contradictions,
so full of reverse logic
that I cannot figure you out.
Can I be blind!

I should realize
that I see you all the time,
you are right before my eyes,
in people,
in creation,

in the wonderful things
(and in the painful things)
that happen to me
and to others around me.

Why should I need to figure you out?
So what if I could?
Would it make you less awesome to me?
Would it make you any less powerful?
Would it make you any less God to me?
Probably not.

I need to let you be God,
and be content with that.
And what contentment it is,
when I surrender my need
to figure things out,
and rest securely in your love and plan for me,
and let you and I do our work.

You are here.
Now. I thank you for that. Amen.

Fifth Sunday of Easter

(A) *Acts 6:1-7*
Psalm 33:1-2, 4-5, 18-19
1 Peter 2:4-9
John 14:1-12

(B) *Acts 9:26-31*
Psalm 22:26-27, 28, 30, 31-32
1 John 3:18-24
John 15:1-8

(C) *Acts 14:21-27*
Psalm 145:8-9, 10-11, 12-13
Revelation 21:1-5
John 13:31-33, 34-35

God,
I see you everywhere,
your presence is anything but containable.

Over and over,
never becoming redundant,
you transform, create,
rearrange and toss around
your goodness
wherever you make yourself known.

Each new creation is unique,

not plagiarized,
a true original.
You have made me unlike any other,
truly amazing, truly you.

May I remember
to feast on the freshness
of your handiwork,
remember that I am wonderfully made,
remember that I am here
in your image.

During this Easter season
and throughout my life,
may I proclaim you alive,
moving and breathing
in me and in everyone. Amen.

Monday of the Fifth Week of Easter

Acts 14:5-18
Psalm 115:1-2, 3-4, 15-16
John 14:21-26

God,
you alone deserve glory.

I sometimes forget this.

I am so needy.
I need affirmation,
I seek recognition.

I am sorry, God,
that I forget about you,
that I often want to steal the spotlight.
You make it easy for me to do so
because you have no ego.
You do not step in and stop me.
You allow me to look foolish in my arrogance.
Thank goodness you forgive me afterwards.

Help me to be released
from the idol of myself;
help me to always honor you
and point others to you
and your wonderful works.

May everything I do in my life bless you.
May I always give thanks to you.
You, God, are my strength and my song! Amen.

Tuesday of the Fifth Week of Easter

Acts 14:19-28
Psalm 145:10-11, 12-13, 21
John 14:27-31

God,
you are my hope and my song,
and how I long to praise you!
But it is difficult to talk openly
to others about you.
I get squeamish and feel funny
talking about you.
I fear that others will think I'm weird,
that they will ridicule me silently.

Yet, I have to remember and realize
that it might just have to be that way
because I cannot help but share
what is so clear to me:
You are here with me,
you are the center of my life,
you are the reason for my happiness.

Help me to have the courage
to always give credit
where credit is due.
Help me to unabashedly
share the good news

that flows from you
and you alone.

Give me the strength
to always tell your glory,
and make known to everyone
just how blessed I am
because of you. Amen.

Wednesday of the Fifth Week of Easter

Acts 15:1-6
Psalm 122:1-2, 3-4, 4-5
John 15:1-8

God,
there are no conditions
for your love for us.
You accept and love me,
no matter what,
and there is absolutely
nothing I can do
that can keep you far from me.

With you there are no hoops
to jump through,
no prerequisites to fulfill
except that I seek to love you
with all my heart,
with all my soul
and with all my strength.

You prune everything that entangles me,
and you replace all confusion in my life
with your clarity.

May I always bear fruit
and be thankful to be your disciple. Amen.

Thursday of the Fifth Week of Easter

Acts 15:7-21
Psalm 96:1-2, 2-3, 10
John 15:9-11

God,
no one can love like you.

I throw these words around so much,
saying them routinely and automatically:
"I love you."
Do I realize what I am saying?
When you say "I love you,"
you mean no holding back,
no strings attached,
no conditions outlined.
You sent your Son
and offered him
as a sacrifice for my failings.
This is the deepest love—
an offering that promises hope
in the midst of hopelessness
and paves the way for me
to move from misery to happiness.

The depth of your love is infinite!
Help me to abide in the same love
that is you.

If we all obey your commandment of love,
your reign will rain on earth.

Fill us with your love. Amen.

Friday of the Fifth Week of Easter

Acts 15:22-31
Psalm 57:8-9, 10-12
John 15:12-17

God,
your love is everlasting.

Sometimes
the initial luster of Easter
can become tarnished for me.

This is supposed to be
an "alleluia" time,
but sometimes I don't feel it.
Instead, I feel out of step with your lead.

Easter is hard
because resurrection
can only make sense
when it appears in the midst
of pain, suffering,
loneliness and isolation.
In other words,
Easter only makes sense
when everything around us
says the opposite.
Your call for me to be

born again
is an invitation to proclaim life
when all other signs
proclaim something else.

Help me to endure
and be a beacon of hope,
especially when I feel afraid,
especially when I am discouraged,
especially when I sense demons dancing within.
Break through, God,
for these are the moments
when we need you. Amen.

Saturday of the Fifth Week of Easter

Acts 16:1-10
Psalm 100:1-2, 3, 5
John 15:18-21

God,
I praise you
for you have created
all that is good.

And yet, if I follow you,
I have to face
some basic consequences:
My life will never be the same.
Because of you,
I cannot go back to the way
things were before.
I have to be willing
to suffer ridicule.
I have to reject values
that I used to embrace.
I have to choose life
over death,
kindness and mercy
over selfishness and greed.
I have to choose you
over the other gods
that want to control me.

The path to you
can be fraught with danger
and unexpected roadblocks.
I need you, God,
to grant me the courage
to run the race—
a real marathon—
and to assure me
that I can count on you
to meet me at the finish line. Amen.

Sixth Sunday of Easter

(A) *Acts 8:5-8, 14-17*
   Psalm 66:1-3, 4-5, 6-7, 16, 20
   1 Peter 3:15-18
   John 14:15-21

(B) *Acts 10:25-26, 34-35, 44-48*
   Psalm 98:1, 2-3, 3-4
   1 John 4:7-10
   John 15:9-17

(C) *Acts 15:1-2, 22-29*
   Psalm 67:2-3, 5, 6, 8
   Revelation 21:10-14, 22-23
   John 14:23-29

God,
in you I find the promise of paradise.

Thank you for all the signs
of your greatness that surround me
and enable me to see
like I have never seen before.
With you I am more focused,
my life is more brilliant and wonderful.
My world is filled
with an everlasting fragrance.
You lead me to a garden

tended by you alone.

When I find you,
you make your ways known to me,
you reveal your justice,
and you continually
forgive and blanket me
with your compassion.

Because of this,
how can I keep from singing?

I have seen you,
I hear your voice,
I know you exist,
and I know that
on the last day,
I, too, will rise again with you.

May everyone I am with today
see you in my words and actions.
May they see what I see—
the glory of God.
May the song burst forth
that you reveal to us a victory,
one that is ours to share. Amen.

Monday of the Sixth Week of Easter

Acts 16:11-15
Psalm 149:1-2, 3-4, 5-6, 9
John 15:26—16:4

God,
I am so thankful for you
for I know you love me
and have sent messengers
to encourage me
on my own journey of faith.

I need your Spirit
to keep me going.
I need your supply of strength,
your inexhaustible well
of courage and light.
In your Spirit
I find the energy
to go the extra miles needed,
to keep my faith fresh
and to sustain my connection to you.

Thank you, God,
for sending us your defender,
and giving us dreams, signs and wonders
that we can witness to.
Thank you for delighting in us,

your children,
your people,
your one body.

Through the power of your Spirit,
there is nothing I cannot accomplish.
As a result,
I have new wings to fly,
new skills for dance
and a stronger voice
when I sing to you!

You alone are the glory of my life! Amen.

Tuesday of the Sixth Week of Easter

Acts 16:22-34
Psalm 138:1-2, 2-3, 7-8
John 16:5-11

God,
I do not have to look
far at all
to know that you alone
can save me.

When I am in need of kindness,
you are there.
When I am surrounded by lies,
your truth cuts through.
When I cry out and no one answers,
you arrive at my front door,
ready to respond
with your wonderful love.

You fill my emptiness,
you endure with me,
you save me with your right hand.

I thank you, God,
for the clarity that you provide.
You prove the values of the world all wrong:
sin, injustice, condemnation.

May I always bank on the hope
that resurrection brings,
and be restored to my youth,
for you call me your child,
precious in your sight. Amen.

Wednesday of the Sixth Week of Easter

Acts 17:15, 22—18:1
Psalm 148:1-2, 11-12, 12-14, 14
John 16:12-15

God,
you always defy the usual,
you always are beyond
our descriptions,
our definitions
and our declarations.

You are you.

Over and over again,
I experience the reversal
of expectations.
You never do the predictable.
I grope for you
and look for you in the things
that make sense to me,
and, of course,
you show up elsewhere.

You cannot be contained
or expressed adequately
in works of art,
in language,

in songs, in poetry and stories,
even in the majesty of your creation.

You are who you are,
and you astound me.

Thank you for the many surprising
and amazing ways
that you become known to me.
Don't stop surprising me
because I love surprises,
especially yours. Amen.

Ascension Thursday

Acts 1:1-11
Psalm 47:2-3, 6-7, 8-9
Ephesians 1:17-23
(A) Matthew 28:16-20; (B) Mark 16:15-20;
   (C) Luke 24:46-53

God,
I want to see the world,
the heavens,
all creation,
in the way that you do.

I need to be enlightened
and led to the vision
that you have laid before me.
I know that you
are the beginning,
middle
and end
of all things.
I want to share
in your heritage.

When I look to the heavens,
I want to see only you.
Help me to look not only up
but around, side to side,

to see the blessings before me.

Jesus ascended to heaven.
Help me to ascend
to the best I can be—
your servant,
committed to bringing you
to all my relationships,
activities and encounters.

Let loose within me, God,
the trumpet blast
that will sound
your joy and glory. Amen.

Friday of the Sixth Week of Easter

Acts 18:9-18
Psalm 47:2-3, 4-5, 6-7
John 16:20-23

God,
you embrace all that I am,
especially my sinfulness,
and make me whole.

You are near to me.
You never leave me alone.
You are with me in all that I do.

I draw on your faith in me, God,
to act courageously
and stay focused on your call
to proclaim your saving power
in every action in my life.
Take my fear and transform my terror
into confidence and faith.
Fill me with new resolve
and determination
to remain with you
and in your ways.

My God, you are wonderful
to choose me

to share in your inheritance.
Thank you for your gift
of love and care. Amen.

Saturday of the Sixth Week of Easter

Acts 18:23-28
Psalm 47:2-3, 8-9, 10
John 16:23-28

God,
you are tireless
in your pursuit of me,
and you ask of me the same:
to reach out to others
and serve them.

This is what resurrection is all about.
It is not only the miraculous event
of the empty tomb
but the unwavering call to us
to go into the world
and deliver the news that anguish,
hopelessness, fear and pain
are not the last word with you.

You have promised all of us
that joy belongs to us.
Whatever we ask in your name,
you will respond,
you will be attentive;
you will not ignore us,
but rather, meet us

with your compassion and assurance
that we belong to you.

Your son, Jesus,
is more than mere memory.
He is with us
now and always.

Help me to always serve your people
and to remember that I am never alone. Amen.

Seventh Sunday of Easter

(A) *Acts 1:12-14*
Psalm 27:1, 4, 7-8
1 Peter 4:13-16
John 17:1-11

(B) *Acts 1:15-17, 20-26*
Psalm 103:1-2, 11-12, 19-20
1 John 4:11-16
John 17:11-19

(C) *Acts 7:55-60*
Psalm 97:1-2, 6-7, 9
Revelation 22:12-14, 16-17, 20
John 17:20-26

God,
I often feel alone
and isolated,
even with those who supposedly
are my friends.

I often feel frightened
and estranged,
sometimes for no apparent reason.
When I feel this way,
I become paralyzed, depressed,
not knowing how to crawl out of the mess.

I feel half-alive.

But you,
you always welcome me.
I am never a stranger to you.
You show me the best hospitality,
with the best flair,
the best sense of wholeness.

Sometimes I am completely baffled
by how good you are to me.
Why do you love me?
What have I done to deserve
your royal treatment?

Thank you for making me
a member of your family
and for giving me a home with you.

Thank you for opening up
the tomb of emptiness
that I feel,
for rolling away the stone
of my fear and despair.

Thank you for not keeping
Easter to yourself. Amen.

Monday of the Seventh Week of Easter

Acts 19:1-8
Psalm 68:2-3, 4-5, 6-7
John 16:29-33

God,
even though I believe in you,
I falter at times
because I want my faith to be easy.
I don't want any complications,
no surprises,
no rocky roads along the way.

I don't want to be
separated from the things
that keep me comfortable
and in control,
that make my environment familiar.
I resist being stretched,
being afflicted.
I want my belief in you
to come with assurances.

You need to break down
the walls around me
that want these assurances.
The only assurance you provide
is your promise to never leave me alone.

You ask me to have faith
especially when I feel tested.
Of course, I have to remember
that this is what faith is:
standing at the edge of a cliff
and trusting enough to take one more step.

Faith is believing
that you will laugh and cry with me
and walk the same lonely roads
that I walk.

Fill me with your Spirit
so I may always be faith-filled. Amen.

Tuesday of the Seventh Week of Easter

Acts 20:17-27
Psalm 68:10-11, 20-21
John 17:1-11

God,
no matter how hard I try,
I cannot escape you.

You show up everywhere,
constantly guiding events,
making things interesting,
and keeping us wondering
what will happen next.

You are at my left, my right,
before me, behind me,
under me, within me,
over me, around me.
You cannot be extinguished.
Jesus found death,
but death could not win.
You are alive!

And so am I,
so what am I to do with that?
You know the answer,
long before I even ask the question.

You reveal your will to me
but I often cannot discern it clearly.

You keep me interested,
anxious, curious
and filled with anticipation.

Open my ears
to the sound of your voice,
that I may hear your truth
and know your plan for me.
Live in my soul
and guide me to build
the temple of your design. Amen.

Wednesday of the Seventh Week of Easter

Acts 20:28-38
Psalm 68:29-30, 33-35, 35-36
John 17:11-19

God,
you implore me
to stay alert,
to remain lucid,
to attend to the movement of your Spirit.

The power and glory
that come from you
do not always come
with a splash,
or in dramatic fashion.
No, you often come in stillness
or in the ordinary
or in the most bland occurrences.

Help me, God,
to recognize you in all things.
Let me be still
to dwell on your word
and what you are saying to me.
Penetrate my clogged heart
and fill my spirit
with your Spirit. Amen.

Thursday of the Seventh Week of Easter

Acts 22:30; 23:6-11
Psalm 16:1-2, 5, 7-8, 9-10, 11
John 17:20-26

God,
you keep me filled
to the brim.
You are all I have
and all I need.

You give me not one day, God,
but a season of Easter
to reflect and revel
in the mystery of your death and rising.
Your Resurrection is my new beginning.
You roll away stones too heavy
for me to shove aside by myself.

You alone, God,
are my portion and cup,
and you have filled me
with a joy that is
unsurpassable,
a joy that seeps into every part
of my being.
It is you that I set before me,
and with you no harm can come to me.

Keep my bowl ever ready
to receive you,
and may my heart
always be pleasing to you,
ready, willing and committed
to do your will. Amen.

Friday of the Seventh Week of Easter

Acts 25:13-21
Psalm 103:1-2, 11-12, 19-20
John 21:15-19

God,
you ask me relentlessly
if I love you.

You ask me to love you
with a love that is most intimate,
a love focused and centered on you
and your will for me.

You ask me to love you
with a love that is other-centered,
that keeps the needs of others
ahead of my own,
a love that is selfless,
a love that serves.

You ask me to love
with a love that is committed
to righting the wrongs
of injustice,
of abuse,
of inequality and hatred,
a love that destroys

all that is evil.

You ask me to love
in ways that reveal compassion,
mercy, forgiveness, acceptance,
and that expose
all that is judgmental,
exclusive and hateful.

Do I love you in these ways?
Not always,
and certainly not enough.
Help my love to be about the truth
and about your purpose. Amen.

Saturday of the Seventh Day of Easter

Acts 28:16-20, 30-31
Psalm 11:4, 5, 7
John 21:20-25

God,
throughout this journey
of Easter,
you have planted in me
a challenge.

You are asking me
to do more than the usual,
annual Easter practices.
You want me
to embrace the waters
of my baptism;
to move outside myself
and make my life
an everlasting gift to you;
to share with others
the eternal and unabashed
story of your rising in me
again and again
and your blinding me
with the brilliance of your light!

You want me to live!

Fully! Not halfway,
not passive,
not with good intentions
and inaction,
not with lip service,
not with melodic, empty alleluias.
You want me to be committed,
invested fully in seeking
the way toward your holy temple,
building your Kingdom,
the city of God
the new Jerusalem,
right here,
right now.

Set me on fire, God,
with your mission
that all will know you
and live forever! Amen.

Pentecost

(Vigil)
> *Genesis 11:1-9; Exodus 19:3-8, 16-20;*
> > *Ezekiel 37:1-14; Joel 3:1-5*
> *Psalm 104:1-2, 24, 35, 27-28, 29, 30*
> *Romans 8:22-27*
> *John 7:37-39*

(Mass During the Day)
> *Acts 2:1-11*
> *Psalm 104:1, 24, 29-30, 31, 34*
> *1 Corinthians 12:3-7, 12-13*
> *John 20:19-23*

God,
you are the great completion
of all our dreams and desires.

By sending your Spirit
to dwell among us,
you opened wide
the promise of new life,
you unleashed the power
of your promise
to soar beyond a single event,
to become a destiny for us all!

With your vision

of life and love
you hold us close,
granting us a share
in your cosmos.
You fill in the gaps
in our lives.
You bust open for all to see
a gift that any other god
would want to hoard
and use to keep us at bay.

But you are different in your ways.
You call us into partnership with you,
with the power of your Spirit,
your breath of life,
you jump-start the dashed hopes of your people.
You gently welcome us as your guests
and hold us with holy sweetness and grace.

Heal my wounds this day, God,
and infuse in me
a new strength,
a new desire,
a new freedom
from my inner and relational slavery
that keeps me bound and trapped.

May every part of my being
proclaim loudly: "Easter!"

God is alive and moving!
God has conquered death!
God is like no other,
for this God calls us
"children of God"!

Keep the muse alive and active,
creating your reign for ever and ever. Amen.